Tutor
and
Grow Rich!

How to make a full time income being a part time tutor.

By Kasey Hammond

www.TutorandGrowRich.com

A special thank you to my husband and best friend Ken for his support, patience and kindness throughout this process together.

Thank you for making me laugh and reminding me of what is important each day.

TABLE OF CONTENTS:

Why start your own home tutoring business?

You will:

- Be your own boss and set your own schedule
- Have more time for family and friends
- Enjoy the benefits of a rewarding and fun job
- Work with children of all ages
- Generate another source of income with very few expenses!

Did you know that:

You have amazing skills that are valuable in the marketplace!

Humans have been tutoring one another since the beginning of history and passing valuable learning to one another. This is a time-tested teaching method that continues to be in demand today!

With NCLB (No Child Left Behind) in place and the

increased expectations of schools, many teachers have additional responsibilities; students can easily fall behind. With national tests and exams, teachers have to spend a lot of time prepping students for these exams and tests.

Parents dream of their child doing well in school, going to college, and starting a successful career, but when they are not doing well in a subject, parents will readily call you for help!

Parents are realizing that their children often need more personalized attention than they are currently receiving from classroom instruction.

Tutoring is an environment without the pressure of peers or any authority and allows the student to freely ask for explanations, learning everything they have struggled with in the classroom.

In today's society, many households have two working parents, leaving little or no time to assist their children in their schoolwork.

Parents wish they could afford private school for their children and choose instead to hire tutors to supplement their education.

Hundreds of thousands of students having difficulty in specific subjects are being tutored in the United States today.

Newsweek Magazine has noted tutoring services as "an exploding market!"

Tutoring franchises sell for a minimum of $20,000 or more + advertising expenses.

Tutoring companies, on average, make about $50 - $70 an hour and only pay their tutors $12 - $16 per hour.

A teaching certificate or Master's Degree is not required to be a tutor.

Many tutors don't have teaching experience yet find many opportunities to teach what they enjoy. If you have the right attitude and enough knowledge, you will find yourself a successful & sought after tutor!

In fact, there are several qualities that are excellent to have before starting your own tutoring business & they aren't learned in a classroom:

- Empathy for your students, knowledge of the subject, enthusiasm and overall friendliness are extremely important qualities in a teacher! I believe that anyone with these qualities will make a VERY successful tutor.

- There are no licensing or state requirements to become a tutor, and chances are you have been a tutor without even knowing it.

- Some tutors start out using tutoring as only a hobby and quickly find that this is a field that doesn't even feel like work. They may find that tutoring on a full time basis is a great fit for them!

- Tutoring is not just a seasonal business based on the school year... students enrolled in summer school need help, and students looking to get ahead and stay current in their work over the summer often call on the help of a tutor!

Who should take advantage of starting his/her own tutoring business?   It's GREAT for:

Moms

Dads

Entrepreneurs

College Students

Teachers

Self Employed Persons

Home schoolers

This program shows you how to market yourself and your skills to:

Teachers

Parents

Schools

School Systems

STEP 1: The first step is to decide with which subject areas and age groups you prefer to work.

You may list yourself as a tutor for all subjects and all ages, but, as with anything, you will soon find that you prefer English versus math (or vice versa) when it comes time to dissect a sentence or solve a very complicated formula. In other words, it is probably best to focus on your areas of expertise. Tutoring will not be fun or enjoyable for you if it is in a subject with which you are not comfortable. Just listen to your heart, and you will know if it is the right subject for you or not!

You may find that a parent who hired you to tutor his child in reading will ask you for additional help in math or science. When the tutor is the right fit for the student, you will be asked to tutor in other subjects that will help you expand your "tutoring resume".

Also, keep in mind that it may be necessary at times to bring your own lessons and/or additional problems and worksheets on the subject you are tutoring, so be sure that you have access to these items (you will find suggestions on how to find these later in the book).

Last but not least, look for other ways to develop your business. Tutoring can easily lead into other avenues for you if you want it to. For example, an English tutor may be asked to do proofreading on the side or editing for local businesses. In this day and age almost everyone has a website that will need editing and proofreading for content.

Businesses also have training for employees in many areas such as motivational training, grammar 101, communication and etiquette as well as computer and programming training.

If you speak a language you can absolutely market yourself to other businesses and do customized language training or translating.

Basically, tutoring can lead you down many paths if you choose to start a successful business. One thing that is VERY important when going out on your own is your reputation. Tutor and Grow Rich will tell you how to make a positive name for yourself as you grow your business.

STEP 2: Getting Started And Marketing Your Tutoring Services.

The first step in marketing yourself is to do a little research. This is easiest to do if you have internet access and use a search engine such as Google or Yahoo. (Keep in mind you can use the internet at your local library- for free!) If you don't have access to the internet, you can also find this information by calling your local county/city information line.

If you are interested in one-on-one instruction, I recommend contacting area school systems. Most areas have what is called a Parent/Teacher Resource Center that compiles a list of tutors and details what subjects/areas you will tutor. This will include your basic contact information.*

Keep in mind that these folks at the resource center are your 'brokers', and that by befriending them and introducing yourself, they are able to put a name with a face when providing your information to prospective clients.

*Note that most school systems require that you complete background check for a small fee. In my area the fee was $5.00, and they required the form to be notarized. (this costs an additional $5.00 at the UPS store or whatever type of store is close to you that has a notary) It was a one time fee and very much worth the cost! Most banks also offer this service at no charge.

Making flyers and putting them in neighborhood paper boxes is also a GREAT way to get your name out there. I printed 100 flyers and delivered them with my husband on a Sunday afternoon in my neighborhood.

Not only did we have fun, but within 24 hours I received a call for a job that was 5 doors down from our house! Flyers are a great marketing tool, relatively inexpensive, and can be done from your home computer. I recommend using colored paper to make them stand out. If you don't want to put them out yourself, there are services who do this on a weekly basis as well as neighborhood kids who could also do it for you. (See my flyer at: www.yourtutoringbusiness.com/flyer.html)

I highly recommend putting your photo on the fliers as it makes your services more personable and gives a professional image. If you do not have a printer or do not wish to pay printing costs, most public libraries allow you to print for free! (Remember to put them in newspaper boxes.)

Good teachers are costly, but bad teachers cost more. ~Bob Talbert

Another recommended step is to have some basic business cards made. (you are now a tutoring professional and need a way to show it!) You can go to an office supply store and buy the pre-perforated business cards and print through a program like Word, or you can also find a website that makes them for very little money.

I found a great company that does the cards for **free**, and they arrived very promptly! You only end up paying the shipping and handling cost! You can also customize them and have your photo added, which again helps personalize yourself and your tutoring business!

Go here to get your 250 cards FREE:

www.yourtutoringbusiness.com/businesscards

In addition to business cards, it is an added bonus (but not necessary) to have your own website.

Nowadays it is fairly inexpensive to register your own domain name. (ex: JanesTutoring.com) I recommend choosing your name as parents and teachers will remember this and happily pass it on to friends.

Register your website domain name here:

www.yourtutoringbusiness.com/website

I have found that parents are impressed by this. Also, if I receive a call and am not available, I can direct them to go to my website to find out more about the services I offer. This presents you as a real person and professional, and the parent will feel more comfortable after reading about your background.

You will need to have a great sales letter on your homepage that tells why your services are unique & details why a student will benefit from your help! For a limited time I am offering FREE revision of your website and sales letter!! My copywriter has agreed to give a limited number of folks a critique, with tips and ideas for writing a winning sales letter! (more on your tutoring website to come in STEP 11)

Once you have business cards made with your website and email address on them, find a list of schools in your area. You can find this information easily on the internet, and if you do not have internet access, look inside the back part of your phone book. The website I found most helpful being in the United States was:

http://www.greatschools.net/

However, doing a quick search online can produce just about any list or name you might need.

By this point you will have most likely narrowed your subject down and, therefore will be marketing certain subjects. For example, I will be marketing to middle and high school teachers since Spanish is not taught until then.

Type your letter to the schools. Introduce yourself, state the purpose of your letter, and provide them with your business card. A great time to do this is after the grading & interim periods.

This is when parents will contact teachers to ask for suggestions/tutor recommendations. You can obtain a report card and interim period typically from the school system's website. (Form letter attached if you wish to use this one.)

You can easily find out the grading periods from your County or City's education webpage.

Sample Letter:

Central High School

Attn: Spanish Department

Ms. Jane Doe

December 1, 2011

Dear Ms. Doe:

Thank you for taking the time to read this letter. I am writing to offer my tutoring services to your school and your Spanish Department. I have worked with many students and teachers in the Richmond area and have assisted in improving student's grades and expectations in their Spanish courses.

I am listed on the Chesterfield County official tutor list, and I also have my own website that details a little more about myself. My website is www.KaseyHammond.com. I am also enclosing some business cards.

Please feel free to contact me if you have any questions or need any reference information. Also, please feel free to provide my contact information to any students you feel could benefit from additional tutoring.

Thanks again, and I look forward to working with you.

Sincerely,

Kasey Hammond

Sign the letter, mail it, and enclose several business cards. I recommend doing this more than once, especially toward the end of the summer and right before the end of a grading period. Don't worry that you are bothering the teacher. Teachers love to receive mail at school that is anything but just the regular junk mail! (Can you relate?)

Usually you can find the faculty list on the internet and address it to the specific head of a department.

If you can't find it, simply call the school and ask the secretary for the first and last name of the head of the department. I recommend addressing it to someone specific to avoid having your letter misplaced or even tossed into the trash. If you are offering tutoring in several different subjects, be sure to send one to each department head.

Also, don't forget private schools! Some of my best clients have come from private schools. The parents are already spending significant money to send their children to school, and the last thing they want is to pay to have the student repeat a subject or a grade!

On the flip side of that, many parents wish they could send their kids to private school but cannot always afford the tuition. They do choose, however, to supplement the public school education with a personalized tutor for their children.

> **What the teacher is, is more important than what he teaches. ~Karl Menninger**

Besides public and private schools, who else needs my services?

If you are more interested in doing group instruction, the following are great markets for small group tutoring.

Most homeschoolers are always looking for additional resources, and this is a great way to move into a small group instruction. In my case, languages are always in demand in this setting, especially Spanish.

Homeschoolers like to get the jump in starting their

children sooner in acquiring a language. Again, use the internet to find local homeschool groups in your area. Most of them have support groups of which many families are members, and, therefore, are another great source of referrals.

Daycare centers are also beginning early in teaching languages and other subjects. Many are willing to pay someone to come in to teach a language, organizational skills, etc. because it makes them more marketable to parents who are shopping for a well-rounded day care program for their children. Children are "sponges" at learning anything we provide them. In my opinion we wait too long in the United States to begin teaching languages to our kids. An example is that I have begun working with my niece in learning Spanish. I have taught her a few songs, and we have done colors and numbers in Spanish. She loves it and is always ready for the next Spanish lesson, and she is only 5!

Community colleges, as well as four-year colleges

are also a great source. Contact them to find out if they have a tutor list, and, now that you have your business cards, you can always leave them on bulletin boards at the library, community colleges, coffee houses, etc. Remember, you are in demand!!

I have received several calls from adults looking for my help in teaching them the basics of Spanish. Oftentimes they are taking a trip to Spain or another Latin American country or just need some basic skills for their job and are looking for someone to work around their schedule!

Also, many adults are looking to develop skills in their career, such as computing or internet skills or maybe even organizations skills!

I had a student's mom ask me to help her organize her kitchen as she was impressed with how I organized my tutoring business! (you never know where tutoring may lead you!)

Newspapers are another great way to advertise. Often times the local community papers are a great source, as they cost very little money and sometimes are even free!   A good ad should be short and simple. I don't think it is necessary to include your rates or unnecessary wording. You may change your rates in the future and therefore you don't want to be locked into a certain price.

Example of ad:

Experienced private tutor offers excellent Spanish tutoring. Call Kasey Hammond, BA Spanish & Latin American Studies, 555-1212

Word of mouth is always the best method of advertising. Once you have tutored a few students and met with success, you will easily find parents are so happy to give out your name and number!

Also, if you belong to a gym or attend a church, these places have bulletin boards for you to put out your cards or your flyers.

Internet Marketing:

Craigslist is a free and can be a very effective way to advertise your tutoring business in your area. Many tutors have great success using CL to advertise their tutoring services. We've all heard about Craigslist scams and scary Craigslist stories so keep this in mind and use common sense when using Craigslist.

If you receive a weird response about someone living overseas whose child needs to be tutored and it seems strange, chances are this is a scam.

Sample Craigslist ad:

Midlothian Spanish Tutor available for one on one or small group instruction for Spanish I -

V. Over 8 years experience and references available. Limited availability! Go to http://www.KaseyHammond.com

Be sure to include the area you live in, the subject and your website. Google will index these ads, which means they'll show up when someone searches in Google as well!

Things to look out for – any responses that ask you to tutor someone who lives abroad or someone who wants to pay you MORE than you are asking or possibly send you a money order – these are all scams and do not require an answer.

List your tutoring business in Google for free.
To do this, you need a free Google account:
Click on the "Maps" tab at the top
Click on the link "Put your business on Google Maps"
Complete the profile and coupon (optional) and you're done!

Social Media:

Facebook has become so popular and I recommend setting up a Facebook Fan Page. You will get a ton of exposure from friends and clients 'liking' your page.

Since you are a tutoring professional, it is best to create a profile page for your business that is separate from your personal profile page. Having separate profiles has its advantages.

A Facebook fan page offers more versatility and is more customizable than a regular profile page. Not only can you use it to market your tutoring services, but you can also deliver valuable information to your potential clients and to provide excellent customer service. Perhaps the biggest advantage of a fan page is that you can have an unlimited number of fans/customers/prospects. This is a great place for building the much-acclaimed email "list". If you do Facebook marketing correctly, you can build a substantial database of followers and a handsome income as a result.

Video Marketing:

With the explosion of YouTube and online video, more and more people are using video to promote themselves and their businesses.

This has helped me dominate Google in my local market.

There are free services to help you like www.TubeMogul.com, but I used a paid service that did all the hard work for me.

You can see it here:

www.yourtutoringbusiness.com/video

Yard Signs

You will want to check your county or city ordinances about the regulations for yard signs but this is a great way to generate instant tutoring leads.   Putting them at busy intersections, close to schools or even by the entrance to family oriented neighborhoods is a great idea.

It is an inexpensive way to advertise and have your phone ringing almost instantly. Putting them out at the beginning of school as well as close to interim and report card time is a good idea. Be sure to post your phone number and website on the yard sign. An inexpensive place to order them is:

http://www.YourTutoringBusiness.com/yardsigns

Other Marketing Resources and Online Tutoring:

There are several directory websites on which you can list your services for very little money. An example of these are the websites listed below:

http://www.TutorPost.com/

http://www.tutornation.com

http://www.directoryoftutors.com/register/

Just remember the secret to good advertising is to make sure that your costs are kept down until you figure out your best advertising source. You will have to find out which is the best source for you in your area. Be sure to ask clients, "How did you hear about my tutoring services?". This way you can find out what advertising is working for you.

You will notice that some of these referral sites offer online tutoring. With the help of technology it is possible to tutor students via the internet and possibly more than one at a time, from the comfort of your own home. Online tutoring is great because you will truly shave off the majority of expenses associated with having a tutoring business.

For example you will not have to drive anywhere and waste time and gas costs as well as paper and books.

Since I launched my tutoring business, I have had the opportunity to network with other tutoring business owners.

I have found a great service that allows you to hold online tutoring sessions directly from your home computer and also gives you the access to an amazing whiteboard system as well as online tutoring leads.

This is yet another added value service that demonstrates your professionalism and how essential you are in the student's learning process. Online tutoring is becoming very popular and allows the student and the tutor to work together despite a snow day or a tutor being out of town, etc.

To profit from online tutoring go here:

www.yourtutoringbusiness.com/online

Licenses/Incorporation/Insurance for your Tutoring Business

Depending on what country, state or county/city you reside in, it may be necessary for you to purchase a business license. In most cases a business license is very inexpensive but may be a requirement you need.

I recommend contacting your local government office to find out if your tutoring business will require having a business license.

I also recommend calling your insurance agent or insurance company and explaining your business. Depending on how you decide to structure your business (where you work from, if you have employees or independent contractors, etc) it may or may not be necessary to purchase an additional policy or additional insurance.

Incorporation may be something you want to consider as your business grows and expands. There are several companies online that offer legal services and can help you get started if you decide to incorporate your business. I recommend and have used the following companies:

www.yourtutoringbusiness.com/incorporate

www.yourtutoringbusiness.com/legal

At some point you may decide to expand your business and hire additional tutors to work for you. Several things to consider are whether you wish to hire them as independent contractors or as direct employees.

There are advantages and disadvantages to both. You will also want to check once again with your insurance company and insurance agent to find out who will be covered by your policy.

Also keep in mind that these additional tutors will be representing you and your company and be sure to hire them wisely and ask them to document each session (see Step 8). It may be necessary to do background checks and screenings on anyone you choose to hire. Several friends and colleagues have recommended hiring a tutor from a website that does background checks. For example, Care.com has tutors list themselves in exchange for submitting to a background check. By hiring tutors from a site like this you can see reviews as well as have a background check already in place.

STEP 3: Pricing Structures And How To Figure Out How Much You Are Worth!

To get an idea of the market, you can simply go to one of the websites above, enter in your location under the *Find a Tutor* section and see what other tutors in the area are charging.

You can also call a company that contracts tutors and ask them how much they charge for tutoring. Two franchised companies that are popular in our area are:

http://www.huntingtonlearning.com/

http://www.clubztutoring.com

Remember, image is everything. Your website, business cards, correspondence and email say everything about you.

A great website and a professional image will ensure that you will be successful and earn $50,$60 & $70 dollars an hour for your services.

Keep in mind that a free, homemade website and business cards will not attract the kind of clients and income you are looking for in starting your tutoring business.

STEP 4: Pricing Guide.

When you set your prices, you need to offer an incentive to pay more money upfront. This will help you receive more money in advance and in the event of a 'no show', you have not lost anything.

When figuring out your pricing structures, don't hesitate to ask for more than other tutors. Remember, you are in demand and they NEED you. Often times, charging slightly more makes the parents really see value in you, and if they feel you are overpriced, then maybe it's best not to work with them.

In creating my pricing model, I also titled them so that the parents could see where their child might fit into the packages. Basically, it doesn't matter which package they choose, as they can use them any way they want in terms of weekly sessions (two per week, etc.)

Here is my model from my website:

Tutoring Services Available:

Maintenance Tutoring, 5 sessions: *$199 ($40/ hour)*

This is for students who want to review concepts as well as review for quizzes and tests on a weekly basis. This is for students who typically have a general understanding of the current concepts but simply need some added review.

Intensive Tutoring, 10 sessions: *$349 ($35/ hour)*

This is for students who have fallen a little behind in their course and need to review past concepts as well as continue learning new concepts.

Super Intensive Tutoring, 20 sessions: *$599 ($30/ hour)*

This is for students who are very behind in their course and who may be failing or are near failing their current Spanish course. This involves intense review of past concepts, preparing for upcoming quizzes and tests and laying out a plan for successful course completion.

Packages are prepaid
By the hour: $50/hour

Another thing to consider is what period of time

equals one tutoring session?

For my subject (Spanish) I have decided that one hour sessions work well. Occasionally I run over the one hour session, but usually the hour is just the right fit for me and for most of my students.

Some subjects may not require that much time. You might only set up your business to use forty-five minute sessions.

Keep in mind that depending on where you are meeting your student, you may need a few minutes to get settled and to pack up.

Deciding whether to charge PER SESSION or PER HOUR is something you should decide right in the beginning. For example, I have always done one hour, so if I try and switch to 45 minute sessions now, the parents might not be too happy with me. I recommend deciding this from the beginning of setting up your business.

For example, either say your price is $50/ session and sessions are generally a 45- 50 minute period. Or, just say you charge $50/hour.

Some tutors prefer having an hourly rate, because that sets a specific period of time for students and parents. That way, if you have chatty parents or students, they might realize that the clock is ticking and that 10 minutes before the session is counting! It's up to you, but this is one of those decisions to make before you start.

If a student chooses a large package (20 sessions or more), you may want to consider slightly longer sessions to be held (for example 1.5 hours). I have found that 1.5 hour sessions really do not require any more work and are a great way to use the student's time effectively and without having to travel as much, therefore keeping costs even lower for you.

Also, the students that buy a large package are usually the ones that need more help and will benefit (at least initially) from spending more time on their subject.

STEP 5: Creating your Tutoring Rules & Regulations.

It sounds too serious, but it is important to have an outline of **do's and don'ts** when you begin. This will allow you to lay out your expectations and will prevent any issues that can possibly arise. The important things to cover are your cancellation policy for the student and his family and also for yourself, should you have to cancel.

In my information sheet I also ask the student and parent to fill out some basic information for me, including the student's name, parent's name, school, teacher, contact info, etc. At the bottom of this sheet I ask them to sign it. I give them a copy and I keep a copy. This ensures that everyone clearly understands what they have agreed to and, once again, it demonstrates professionalism. Clearly delineated guidelines and rules always make people feel comfortable when contemplating starting something new! (as you know by purchasing this ebook!)

(My information sheet is attached. Please note where mine says Spanish Level, yours might say Course or Subject for general purposes.)

Also, decide what your billing preference is from your students and parents. For example, do you wish to invoice your client's weekly/monthly or will payment be due at the beginning or end of session? If so, will you email or mail out these invoices?

I prefer to get paid up front at the beginning of each session so that I do not have to mail invoices. I accept checks and cash of course and can accept credit cards through my Pay Pal account when necessary. You can provide this link when you email out your information sheet to parents or when you send your Lesson Summary.

Tutoring Services Available:

Maintenance Tutoring, 5 sessions: *$199 ($40/ hour)*

This is for students who want to review concepts as well as review for quizzes and tests on a weekly basis. This is for students who typically have a general understanding of the current concepts but simply need some added review.

Intensive Tutoring, 10 sessions: *$349 ($35/ hour)*
This is for students who have fallen a little behind in their course and need to review past concepts as well as continue learning new concepts.

Super Intensive Tutoring, *$599 ($30/ hour)*
This is for students who are very behind in their course and who may be failing or are near failing their current Spanish course. This involves intense review of past concepts, preparing for upcoming quizzes and tests and laying out a plan for successful course completion.

Sessions paid by the hour: $50/hour

Payment For Lessons

The full fee for each lesson is to be pre-paid and is due at the beginning of the lesson. You may use cash, check or money order to pay the tutoring fee. If you pay by check or money order, please make it payable to Kasey Hammond.

Canceling or Changing Lessons

If you ever need to cancel or change a tutoring appointment, please contact me directly, no later than 4 hours before the session. For example, to cancel or change a lesson scheduled for Wednesday at 7 pm, please contact me no later than 3 pm.   If the lesson is not canceled or rescheduled within a 4-hour period I will ask to be compensated for the lesson.

Lesson Summary Report

After each tutoring session, I will provide a summary report of what the goals were for the session as well as what was completed and what needs to be completed (homework). I will email (or mail if necessary) these to you so you can stay current with what your student is working on.

Please complete the following

Student's name:

Student's grade & school:

Teacher's name and email:

Subject and Level:

Area student needs assistance:

Parent's name:

Address:

Home Phone:

Work Phone / Cell Phone:

Parent Email:

**Does your child have any Medical Conditions I need
to be aware of?

Organization is a huge part of running any business, especially your successful tutoring business!

It is necessary to maintain an updated client list and have it with you at all times in case you need to re-schedule or change times with one of your students.

If you are a cell phone user, you might consider entering everyone's phone numbers into your phone so you can reach students and parents by phone or by text. I have a system that I have set up that helps me juggle all my students in what is (usually) a pretty organized way!

I have a very large, three ring binder. I have tabs

for all of my student's with their individual names on it. At the beginning of each student's name I have a basic document I call a session log. It contains the student's name, address, phone number, Spanish level and teacher. The remainder of the page has these headings:

Student's Name:

Address:

Phone Numbers:
Teacher:
Subject and Level:
Session Log:

Date	Location	Time	Pay
May 5th	Midlo Library	1-2	$40

Under each of these I record the information at the beginning of each of our session. That way I have it with me at all times and can quickly refer to it and keep up with payment and sessions remaining if they have purchased a package. Parents often ask me how many sessions are remaining and that way I can always pull out my book and let them know.

Once my parents have filled out the Student Information sheet, I make a new tab in my tutoring folder, print a name label and fill out my student's contact info. I also put any lesson activities or resources that the student might need during our sessions. This is just one way to organize.

Some tutors prefer to have a separate file folder for each of their students with their info in it. Find a method that is simple and you can access easily. Keep in mind sometimes students cancel or you see students that you weren't expecting to see, so it is helpful to have all your students with you at any time.

Notice on my Information Sheet I have a question about medical conditions. This is VERY important. I recently had a student who I did not know had epilepsy. We were in the middle of a tutoring session when he had a seizure. It was very scary. If I had known about his epilepsy, then I would have been more prepared. Luckily I was immediately able to reach his mom and find out what to do.
However, I learned the hard way that I need to be prepared in these situations as the tutor and adult.

STEP 6: You've Just Received Your First Phone Call To Tutor!

You are very excited...but now what?!

Rules for the first tutoring inquiry.

Rule #1: Ask how they heard about you. This will be important if you choose to have a referral program as discussed later in the book. It is also important if you have paid for any advertising in a local newspaper to see if the ad is working for you!

Rule #2: Ask lots of questions about the student over the phone. Find out in what areas he/she is struggling, how he is studying currently, what his current grade is, and what the expectation is. I have found that if the student has an *F* and the parents call me in May with the hopes of his/her passing the course by the end of the school year, I may not want to work with the student (or the parents). With unrealistic goals, the parents want you to be a miracle worker rather than a tutor, and this places too much pressure on you.

Rule #3: Tell them a little bit about yourself and your background. Let them know about yourself and your tutoring experience. (Keep in mind, to tutor is "To have the guardianship or care of; to teach; to instruct.")* These are things we do every day in our daily lives! You have informally been a tutor your whole life...when you give someone directions, by definition, you are acting as their tutor!
courtesy of Merriam-Webster's online dictionary

Rule #4: Don't sound too eager. Tell them that you have a little more information that you would like them to read and look over as well as your 'tutoring guidelines'. It is easiest to email this to them, but it can also be mailed or faxed. Ask them to look it over, discuss it with their child and for them to give you a call to schedule a session if they decide that tutoring is right for them.

Some parents may want to set up a session immediately. This is great too; however, still send them the information so they can bring it to you at your first session.

Most parents will let you know if their student has an IEP or learning disability, which is important to know ahead of time, as it affects how you will work with the student. Ex: if the student has an IEP (individualized education plan) due to memory issues, ADHD, etc., suggest the parent have index cards available for you and your student to make flash cards so the student has access to a quick study guide to review in between sessions. You may also ask to see a copy of the IEP so that you can see what the student is allowed to have to supplement his or her disability.

Also, keep in mind that you **MAY NOT** wish to work with this parent and student. Tutors are not miracle workers, so it is good if in this initial conversation you can obtain a clear outline of the long term and short term goals of the parent and student.

For example, if the student is currently failing and the parent is expecting them to have an A within the next 30 days, then this may not be realistic and therefore you may not wish to work with the student and parent as their expectations are unreasonable.

Every parent and family is different and has different expectations and therefore this initial phone call is the opportunity for you to ask questions and outline what the parent and student are looking to receive from you. For example, one family I tutor for is thrilled if their daughter brings home C's in Spanish. On the other hand, I have several other families that expect nothing less than an A or a B from their child.

The student will definitely benefit from your help but keep in mind the student will only succeed if they are willing to put forth the effort. Again, tutors are not miracle workers!

Rule#5: Let them know where you would like to work. If you would like to drive to their home, meet at the public library or in your home. Most of the tutoring chains require that the tutor go to the student's home and have an adult over the age of 18 there or else go to a public facility such as the library or their school.

Tutoring in your own home is great because it allows you to book back-to-back sessions. If someone is a no-show, then you can continue to go about your day with little time lost. It also helps reduce gas costs and doesn't require you to waste the down time it takes you to drive from place to place. (Note that most tutoring companies recommend that a parent of someone age 18 or older attend the session along with the student. Use your best judgment.) Also, you may want to contact your insurance agent about your homeowner's policy to be sure that you would be covered in the event of any accident, etc.

If you are doing online tutoring, then insurance isn't a problem! You can work from home with no worries about cleaning your house!

I have a library about 5 minutes from my house. Most libraries have several small rooms available for reservation called Study or Tutor Rooms. My preference is to meet my students at the library where I will book back to back sessions. This limits my travel time and also allows me to easily book 5-6 sessions a day.

Some schools have study halls so you can go and meet with your students during study halls in an empty classroom or in the school library. I find this very helpful in that you might tutor in the morning and free up your evening and afternoons for more students.

Rule #6: Let them know that you would also like to be in contact with the student's teacher so that you can get an idea of what areas the teacher feels the student needs help. This is a great way to develop a relationship with the teacher, which will be very valuable down the road (See referrals further in the book).

I have parents emailing me to find out what the teacher said about their student! (It sounds strange, but it is amazing how quickly parents will come to depend on you!)

Rule #7: In your email/mail to the parent, thank them for the call, express gratitude for contacting you, and provide once again your contact information along with your Outline of your Tutoring Rules/Guidelines (or whatever you choose to title it!)

> **You have powers you never dreamed of. You can do things you never thought you could do. There are no limitations in what you can do except the limitations of your own mind.**
>
> *Darwin P. Kingsley*

STEP 7: You've Scheduled Your First Lesson.

The first session typically flies by! You are meeting your student, possibly his or her parents, and the first part of the session needs to be about your getting to know them. Ask questions, let them know they can ask you anything, and there are no right or wrong things they can ask while you work together. (academically speaking)

This is a great time to become familiar with the textbook they are using, analyze his or her skill level and make an assessment on where you think the student needs to be, as well as a basic plan for how he/she can advance. Sometimes this involves significant review and meeting several times with you per week.

Other times it involves the student's committing to independent study for **x** number of hours in addition to meeting with the tutor. Oftentimes the teacher or school has a weekly review or tutoring session that you recommend the student attend in addition to your sessions together.

Ask your student questions about his/her test taking skills:

Are you the first / last to finish a test? Do you prefer fill in the blank or multiple choice? This will give you an insight into how he/she prepares currently and, more importantly lets you know how to better prepare them.

Also, ask them for a recent quiz or test. This will give you an idea of where the breakdown may be so that you can make suggestions. Example: One of my students was rushing through tests and not proofreading to correct silly mistakes, such as missing accent marks. Together, we developed rhymes and memory tricks, so that he was able to complete his test and then go back using our memory tricks and mark all the accents in the correct places.

You won't believe how honest kids will be with you. I have had students tell me that they don't turn in their work. Sometimes they forget, sometimes they don't do it and sometimes they just need a cheerleader. (That's where you come into the equation). Once your student starts doing better in that class you will notice that they will become more motivated to complete their work and will actually want to do it because they understand it now!

STEP 8: What To Do After The Lesson.

After the lesson it is very important to document the session. You need to document everything from the time you met, the place, the date, the goals for the session, what was accomplished, the student's participation, recommended assignments and any other related comments. (sample template attached.)

SAMPLE Lesson Summary for Jane Doe

Date & Time:

 12/2/07 8-9 pm

Subject:

Spanish III

Location:

Public Library

Session # 1 of 5

Payment: 40.00 paid by check

Overall Goal:

To improve Spanish level III grade from a D to passing; Jane and I discussed ways to study vocabulary in the future through the use of flash cards, as well as getting a general understanding of Jane's current comprehension of the vocabulary, written stories, and questions.

Lesson Plan:

Reading and translating paragraphs in her textbook, identifying vocabulary words, picking out the verbs, identifying the tense and the person.

What was completed:

We read the translation on page 124 in Jane's book and reviewed the vocabulary words, and I asked Jane to identify several different verbs. We reviewed the concept of indirect and direct objects and made flash cards for any vocabulary that Jane did not know.

Feedback:

Jane was very easy to work with and knew most of

her vocabulary by the end of our session.

Homework & Review:

Review vocabulary and study flashcards!

Miscellaneous Notes:

This was the first session that was set up for me to tutor Jane. Jane seems to have overall knowledge of the subject but is lacking in discipline in her study skills. She indicates that she does not study much at all. I think with adequate tutoring and Jane's studying and reviewing on her own, she can easily achieve a passing grade in this Spanish III class. If you wish to continue, please contact me for availability. Thank you!

This lesson summary is not only important for your records, but also important for you to send to the parents. This will reinforce your importance, validate your costs, and summarize what was done in your tutoring session. It will also let the parents know that you do have recommended activities that you want to see completed. It is easiest to email, but it can also be mailed.

Some tutors prefer to do monthly summary reports or progress reports. I think this is a great idea too, however, I would rather write them when they are fresh in my mind and then I can review them right before an upcoming session to remind myself what we worked on last time and what chapter the student was on, etc.

Once you write a few lesson summaries it will become very easy, and you can almost complete them in your sleep!

Some tutors I know will jot down notes at the end of

their session on a form similar to above and then hand it to their student as they are leaving the tutoring session. This is a quick way to also do the same thing; however, you will not have a copy for your records if you need to reflect back on your notes.

Tip: Don't reinvent the wheel!

There are so many websites out there that have supplemental activities to use with your students depending on your subject, and most are free!

The one I have found that works for my Spanish tutoring is:

www.studyspanish.com

I found this site by simply looking through Google. They have hundreds of awesome lesson plans available at no cost!

A website I found for more elementary math is

For all Subjects, I found http://www.syvum.com

In addition to using additional outside resources, most school systems use the same book. You may either buy your own set from the publisher, or once you have become acquainted with some of the teachers, they are usually more than happy to let you borrow one of their extra books for the school year.

Having the actual book is a great way to stay current with what your students are working on and how they are progressing, but it isn't absolutely necessary.

The newer books almost all have a companion website with additional quizzes online, tests & information. These websites are great and allow you to bring additional review material to the session without having to do too much outside work.

Find out the student's book and then simply go online, typing in the name and publisher into Google. Chances are, you will find it easily. An example of this is McDougal Littell.

Their companion website is www.Classzone.com

They have great supplemental exercises for all subjects here.

STEP 9: Stay In Touch with Everyone!

Periodically email or call the teachers and ask how the student is doing in his or her subject. This will remind the teacher to keep you in the loop as to test and quiz schedules. I have one teacher who emails almost weekly to let me know when the next quiz or test is or else how the student did on his or her last quiz or test.

The teachers are typically so grateful to have someone who is also trying to help the student that usually they are VERY helpful in assisting your efforts.

It also reinforces your value once again to the parent. Frequently, the parents have hired you because they do not have the time nor knowledge of the subject. Therefore, you are helping them by staying in touch with the teacher and staying on top of their child's subject and grades. By doing this you will become an integral part of the teacher and student relationship and parents will come to depend on you and you will continue to assert your important role.

STEP 10: How To Get Referrals And What To Do When You Get One!

A referral incentive program is a great way for parents to spread your name into the community. Example: If the student/parent recommends you to another student, give the recommending parent/student a free regular session or a free thirty minute session. This will create more money for you in the long run and gives them reason to recommend you to even more of their friends and family!

These folks are also good sources to list as references and testimonials in your information sheet. You may have a potential client who would like to speak with someone before hiring you. These references are an excellent source of marketing for you!

As you can see, if you are successful in creating a relationship with the teachers, they will be one of your most productive sources of marketing, and, best of all, it is FREE! As soon as I hear that a teacher has recommended me or given my name to someone, I immediately send a handwritten thank you note. In these times of email, handwritten notes go a long way. Remember to express your gratitude and to include a few more business cards!

I have found a great website that I can input all my student and teacher's mailing addresses. It makes it so simple and easy to send out a personalized card through the internet.

It also reminds me when it is one of my student's birthdays or graduation.

I have come to use this site so much, not only for my business, but also for friends and family members to send out birthday and holiday cards. Go to:

http://www.AmazingFollowup.com/

For certain teachers that I work with often, I like to send them something around the holidays, whether it is a small gift basket or a holiday card to let them know I appreciate their business and their support. Again, these small expenses will MORE THAN PAY for themselves in the long run! (and they are heartfelt!)

STEP 11: Your Tutoring Website!

It is important to have a professional and quality website that will help sell your services. Thanks to trial and error I now I have a website that helps me attract new clients and gets great SEO (search engine optimization) but it wasn't always this way. I have a funny story to share...

My first attempt at a tutoring website flashed an ad that I had puppies for sale! This is a true story. It's kind of embarrassing but I should share it. When I first got started in the tutoring business I knew it was important to have my own website. Not knowing anything about creating websites and web pages I used a site that advertised free websites.

I was very excited and quickly created my free website. Shortly afterward I received a call from a lady that I thought was a potential client. They first said they saw my website (I got excited- hot fish on the line!) Then the lady asked me if I still had puppies for sale and how much they were? Huh?

Bottom line I realized after some back and forth with the caller that my 'free website' had the ability to flash ads and spam junk across my website. Can you believe it? Somehow this lady had gotten to my site and contacted me when she saw an ad about puppies. I was mortified and ashamed to tell my husband who at that time worked for an internet company. But reluctantly I did and that's when everything changed for the better!

At that time, I was an internet newbie. I had no idea what to do, where to start or how to even have my own website. I could email and go to websites but that was about it for me. Luckily I had an internet guru who helped me get my website up and running and position myself to get awesome results in Google.

As a newbie to the internet I wasn't sure what it would cost. I could have easily shelled out thousands of dollars for a website and never known I was being ripped off.

If you already have a website but aren't getting a lot of traffic or converting leads into clients then skip ahead to find out how you can convert those leads into high paying customers!

Free site vs. paid site?

Well, you've heard my story and how I learned my lesson the hard way using a "free" hosting site. We've all seen that you can have a free website and not pay for anything. But if you are doing this now or considering it, just keep in mind that you can not control the ads running on the pages or the junk flashing across the screen. You might give your business card out to a potential client and then they go to your site only to see weird ads on your site and they would assume you put those up there. Not a good idea….Spend the extra money to look professional and control all content on your site.

Choose a domain name.

First, decide what you want your website name to be. This is called a domain name. When choosing your domain name it is best to incorporate your name into your domain. For example my website is my name: KaseyHammond.com but if your name isn't available then it's a good idea to include your geographic area in your name. For example RichmondSpanishTutor.com or SeattleMathTutor.com

As I have mentioned, registering a domain name is cheap and varies in price but roughly it will cost you $10.00 – $15.00 per year. Don't choose a .net or .biz   It's just simpler to choose a .com domain name and most people will assume that your site is a .com anyway.

We like to use this service for a domain name:

YourTutoringBusiness.com/website

Hosting your website.

In order for your website to be live and active, you will need to choose a hosting company. Hosting is not very expensive and for an average website should cost less than $10 a month.

You can host with the same company as your domain name if you want, but it's recommended to host with a company that doesn't control your domain name as well.

After using several different hosting services over the years, the one that stands out for reasonable pricing and amazing customer service is:

YourTutoringBusiness.com/hosting

Choose Your Website Theme and Design.

If you haven't heard already... the best software to design and publish your website is totally FREE! And it's called Wordpress.

Here's why you want to use WordPress as your website platform:

Massive choice of themes – WordPress comes with two default themes (themes control the look and feel of your site) already installed which are quite basic, however there are thousands of free themes available.

Fantastic functionality – You don't need to be a programmer or know any php coding to adjust your WordPress installation, everything you need to do can be done via the dashboard. Create posts, pages, pictures and graphics, audio, and video and so on.

Extendability with thousands of plug ins – There are nearly 8,000 plug ins available that you can install to enhance the usability and functionality of WordPress. Again these are easily searched, installed & activated via your dashboard. Some popular plug in additions, improve seo, enhance blog comment functions, page orders, twitter tools, xml sitemap creators, pinging, rotating tag clouds... the list is endless.

SEO friendly – The structure of the WordPress is such that it is optimized for search engines "out of the box". The mere process of blogging and creating fresh content is something the search engines love. However with the installation of one plug in "All In One SEO Plug In" the site will be fully optimized, taking away the mystery of SEO which is so often made to look so much more complicated than it actually is.

Here's how to install:

1) Log into your cPanel (control panel).

2) Scroll down until you're near the bottom of the page.

3) Locate the section entitled "Software/Services."

4) Click on the Fantastico icon. It's the one with the blue smiley face.

5) On the Fantastico page, click the "Wordpress"

text link on the left sidebar.

6) Click on "New Installation"

7) Choose which domain you want this Wordpress install to be on. If you've got an individual site hosting plan, this will default to your one domain. If you have a shared hosting plan, choose which domain you want this Wordpress install to be on.

In the section that says, "Admin access data," is where you'll put the login name and password you want to use to log into your Wordpress blog dashboard.

8) Fill in the "Base Configuration" fields with the name you want to be associated with all the posts you write in your new blog. Also, add in your email address and the website's domain name for your new blog.

9) Click "Install Wordpress."

10) You will be given the domain information, to make sure that it's being installed on the correct domain. If it looks good, click "Finish Instillation."

You're done. You've just installed Wordpress on your new tutoring website. Make sure to write down your login information and/or print out the information on the screen so that you can remember how to log in so that you can access your new blog.

Website Content.

Keep in mind your website content is the first thing that potential clients will see. You want it to be interesting and entice them to take action! Having several testimonials on your main page from success stories is highly recommended to pre-sell clients on the value and importance of your services.

Also it's a good idea to have your photo and even a video or audio of yourself talking on the main page. It helps to personalize your business and clients immediately feel as though they know you.

You should have a short bio on yourself. Some people chose to make a separate page for your bio or an "About Me" page. Either way it's important to talk briefly about your education and experience and also add something personal. Don't include a copy of your resume but keep it light and again use this opportunity to personalize yourself so that you seem fun, easy to work with and encouraging.

I've already mentioned the importance of testimonials. A testimonial is a favorable review of your services from a satisfied client. These can act as your references if you wish or you can also have a separate web page for references. If you are including the name and city/ state of your testimonial that should be adequate but some tutors will also have a special page for references.

You will want to include your rates on your website. Some clients will go to your website, see your rates and you will never hear from them again. Don't worry! That just means your website is doing it's job of filtering out the clients that you don't want anyways. I recommend having packages as well as an hourly rate, but it's up to you, I think clients like to have options so on my website I have several different pricing options.

If you feel the need to add more photos or graphics to your site, a great resource we use is: BigStockPhoto.com where you can search by keyword for the perfect images for your new site. It is affordable and offers professional images at a reasonable rate.

Getting Great Search Engine Results.

You want your tutoring site to come up on the first page of Google when potential clients do a search. For example if someone types in Calculus Tutor Richmond, Va you want your name to pop up as #1! Once parents click on your link they will mentally know that you came up on the first page of Google and will equate that with success.

A good idea is to name your main page of your website what you think parents will search for. For example my main page is titled " Richmond's Spanish Tutor"and it helps me get leads from all over our city.

To get free traffic from Google, be sure to list your business in Google Places. To do this you just need to have a free Google account.

Click on MAPS at the top of the page

Click on Put My Business on Google Maps

Complete the profile and you are done!

Use the power of Craigslist the smart way. Post an ad with your subject and geographic location in the title. For example "Richmond Algebra Tutor"

This is an easy way to get more website traffic and come up on the first page of Google. I am sure you are aware that you might have to filter out a little spam from Craigslist but it's just another way to drive traffic to your site.

If you are using any tutoring directories such as TutorPost.com or TutorsTeach.com, be sure that you can tag your posts and include your city and state in the title of your ads. This will continue to help you get great search engine results.

Overall Website Appearance

Your website serves two purposes initially: it makes you appear like a tutoring professional and it gives parents a way to contact you.

Be sure to keep your website simple enough that the primary goal is clear. (securing new clients)

After you have secured that person as a client then you might consider having a member's page where you give tips or ideas for parents. You might also consider having products for sale that you recommend. (whether it's your own product or you are promoting someone else's product as an affiliate)

You may also want to set up an email system that is automated. (See Resource Page) You could send out reminder emails about upcoming tutoring appointments. Send out broadcast messages regarding holiday schedule or closings for weather. You could also use your email to market your products and services or promote a special offer or upcoming special class or camp.

Website Do's and Don'ts.

Okay, we are positive people so let's start with the Do's!

DO: Have a short bio on yourself and a recent photo of yourself and any tutors who work with you.

DO: Use audio and video to personalize yourself and your business.

DO: Make your contact information very easy to find.

DO: Use testimonials front and center on your

home page.

DO: Clearly highlight your tutoring rates so there is no question how much you charge.

DON'T: Use a 10 year old photo of yourself on your website. We know you looked great, but let's be real!

DON'T: Have 8 paragraphs about yourself bragging about all your accomplishments. Parents want someone qualified but they also want a tutor that their kids will be able to relate to during their sessions.

DON'T: Have any links that point away from your site, you want them to take one action and one action only... call you to book a session!

DON'T Have a testimonial from your husband or wife or anyone who shares your same last name. It doesn't look professional.

Website STEP 9: What are you waiting for? Take

action!

Now is the time to get your website operating at full capacity for you and for your tutoring business success. You can do it. I believe in you! I once knew nothing about websites but I did know that to be professional and stand out I needed to capitalize on having a website that would also drive traffic and leads to me.

Again, you don't have to be a programmer, you don't have to know PHP or any other weird languages. All you need is to get the ball rolling! And once you do....see STEP 10!

Website Critique.

I mentioned earlier that my copywriter would give you a free website review. Now is the time to get a professional's opinion on how to make your site work even better. Contact me at kasey@yourtutoringbusiness.com for more info.

STEP 12: Potential "Pitfalls."

Okay, so I have been singing the praises of tutoring throughout this book, and 98% of tutoring is fun and easy. There are a few things to look out for, though, and unfortunately I had to learn a few lessons the hard way. I lost money in a few situations, and my feelings were hurt on more than a few occasions!

#1: Missed Sessions: There will be occasions when your student will just simply not show up, or he will call you five minutes before the scheduled session to cancel.

This can be handled in several ways, and I have handled it in different ways depending on the student. If you have a package plan and they have purchased and pre-paid a package, then just simply deduct a session from them.

If you decide not to have packages and charge on a per hour/ per visit, then you may want to consider asking for a deposit from the parent before you ever meet so that you still get paid when they miss a session or cancel at the last minute. This is good incentive for them and a gentle reminder that missing a session still means they must pay you!

Occasionally, if it is a true emergency and I didn't waste gas driving, I will reschedule with the student and not charge anything.

#2: Teachers

I had been tutoring for about 8 months before I ever had a "problem teacher." Up until this point I had wonderful success working with the teachers. I contacted a teacher to introduce myself, inquire about the student I was going to be working with, and to find out what they were working on, areas the teacher thought needed improvement etc. and here was my response, "Who are you and what are

YOUR qualifications to work with my student?"
Yikes!!

At first my feelings were quite hurt...I sent a very polite email back explaining my background and how the parent had contacted me to provide extra help to the student and to prepare him before tests and quizzes, etc. I NEVER received an email back from the teacher.

Shortly afterward, the parent of the student emailed me to ask me not to contact the teacher as she had given her son detention two days in a row. She felt the teacher was threatened by his working with a tutor and was taking it out on her son!

I will let you draw your own conclusions about this teacher! I guess on a positive note for us, this is why tutoring has become such a BOOMING business!

Other tutors I know have met with similar responses

when contacting teachers. Don't let it discourage you! It's like anything in life- some teachers will be VERY receptive and others will be negative and try and tell you why it will not work. Keep smiling and being the great tutor you are. You will continue to be successful.

 Since this initial incident, I have learned not to take it personally and move on with improving my student's development! (and being a positive person in his or her life!)

#3: Time

The great thing about owning your own tutoring business is that you can choose when you want to work. When you are working mostly with school aged students then you are somewhat limited to working around their school and sports schedule.

It is pretty inevitable that you will choose to work

some evenings and weekends. The good news is that most students have a study hall at their school, and I have had great successes in meeting them during this period. This has proven to be a great benefit in that, if their study halls are in the morning, I can go and tutor one or two students back to back and make room for more students in the evening schedule.

I have found that most schools are open to this and that the parents are delighted, as it means less shuffling and driving around for them. In fact, one of the private schools I work with brags to parents that "Kasey will come over to our school during study hall and is here on most Tuesdays and Wednesdays.'

The school above is a private school and I have found that working with private schools is wonderful! They don't have as many rules, are open to suggestions and ideas and want their students to succeed and therefore will recommend you to parents.

Also, usually you will not have parents who are trying to bargain with you about your rates. Most private school parents understand that a good education and a good tutor do cost money!

STEP 13: GROWING PAINS.

If you are a successful tutor chances are that you will reach a point in your business after a year or fifteen months where you will have growing pains – this is a good problem to have! You will have more clients than you can fit into your schedule.

You will have to make a decision on how to handle this. You can raise your rates so that you will be getting more per hour and therefore you'll be tutoring less students. Some parents won't be able to pay the higher rate and therefore you will be able to work with the parents and students who are able to pay the higher rate.

You can start a waiting list and work them in over time if you have a client stop attending or go to only meeting on a less regular basis. The negative to this is that if you can't fit them in quickly enough you may lose this client to another tutor.

The other option is hiring other tutors to work for you. There are positive and negatives to this. Obviously it allows you to continue earning money even when you aren't working, but you will be putting your reputation on the line and company name, therefore you will want to hire very carefully. Depending on what works best for you, these are things to consider as your business begins to grow.

STEP 14: Last but not least....HAVE FUN!

A successful tutor and someone who is successful in any type of business is someone who enjoys what they do. For me, tutoring is not anything remotely like work. I look forward to each and every student and every hour we spend together. If you are tutoring properly and tutoring the correct subject for you, it will probably never feel like work.

Meeting new people should be a fun experience. Get to know your students...send them and their family holiday cards, let them know a little bit about yourself, find out who their favorite team is, find out their birthdays and send them a card. Several of my students gave me Christmas gifts this year and I received cards from almost all of them! One of the gifts was a beautiful watch with a card that read, "We appreciate all the **time** you spend with Andrew." Tutoring in a one-on-one situation or small group tutoring is the ultimate teaching environment (no discipline problems, no extracurricular responsibilities, no endless paperwork.)

Also, I have found that all my students have made an impact on me. They have tutored me on things and I have learned about subjects I knew nothing about. For example, one of my students is a karate champion and recently won a national championship!

It has been fun & exciting to learn about this sport and to follow his career. In addition, you may find a barter system will work in your business too. For example, my husband and I argue about mowing the lawn and whose turn it is to mow it every summer!

So, this year, I decided to be proactive and I asked one of my student's if in exchange for 2 sessions of tutoring he would mow our lawn for the month! He said sure and his parents were thrilled to save the money!

If you are an introvert, it is sometimes harder to have a good time and view meeting new people as a 'fun' experience. The more you do this, the easier it will become. Not only are you making a difference in how someone views a certain subject, you are also shaping how the students will view themselves. Building people up is always more fun than tearing them down, so always try and leave the session on a positive note. You will feel happier as a result and get more calls... After all, who wants a grumpy tutor?

Resources Page:

1. Business Cards:

To receive your 250 free cards, click on the following link:

www.yourtutoringbusiness.com/businesscards

2. Website Information:

To register your own domain name and get information about website design, click on the following link:

www.yourtutoringbusiness.com/website

3. Online Tutoring:
www.yourtutoringbusiness.com/online

4. Free Website Review & Critique:

I have arranged for my website designer and copywriter to give you a free review and critique of your new website! This is valued at $250.

Email me at kasey@yourtutoringbusiness.com to get more details.

5. Quickest and easiest way to create your professional website:

www.yourtutoringbusiness.com/websoftware

6. For an automated system to send out thank you cards instantly through the mail:

www.AmazingFollowup.com

7. Tutor Directory for Advertising to Students:

www.TutorPost.com

8. Incorporation and Legal Help:

www.yourtutoringbusiness.com/incorporate

www.yourtutoringbusiness.com/legal

9. Yard Signs:

www.yourtutoringbusiness.com/yardsigns

10. Website hosting:

www.yourtutoringbusiness.com/hosting

11. Automated Email System:

www.yourtutoringbusiness.com/email

Questions and Answers.

The following questions and answers are direct excerpts from our forum, MyTutorSpace.com. MyTutorSpace.com is a place for tutors all over the world to share their thoughts, ideas as well as brainstorm and collaborate with other successful tutors.

A quick thank you to all the awesome members we have on this forum who make it an awesome place to get ideas and answers!

Q: Best and Cheapest Advertising and Marketing?

* Posted by Diana on August 12 at 6:03pm

Well, it has taken quite a bit of time and planning over the past several months, but I'm finally ready to roll. My website is up and running, although I have yet to get my first client...which brings me to my question. I'm looking for cheap and effective ways to market my business. I would love some suggestions for online marketing as well as other types of advertising that have worked well for you.

A: Reply by H. D on August 13 at 11:39am

I have had success with the following advertising: care.com , sittercity.com, wyzant.com (be careful with this one, they take a % of what you make, but they have extremely high search results so it can be worth it); yard signs, especially near schools; postcards (I drive around and put them on mailboxes- it's only worth it if they're the on the street kind. It seems to me that the more expensive advertising does no good.

I have tried advertising in print and on websites like patch.com, as well as sponsoring various things, but I haven't gotten clients that way. It may be worth doing Google adwords at first. I got a fair amount of traffic this way, but it got very expensive. The keywords I wanted in my area got up to $70/month. Wait until they send you a free credit and then sign up, you can get $100 that way. Also, watch ask the training videos they have so you make an effective campaign.

Reply by Lynda on August 14 at 9:16am

My current best form of advertising is word of mouth. But when I first got started it was yard signs. I am also a member of Care.com but have never received any clients from them. Also I advertise on Yahoo, Google, Yellowpages, Bing, etc. - all for free.

Reply by Kasey Hammond on August 17 at 3:45pm

Hey Diana, I posted flyers at my library and our town's grocery store. You might also try local gyms or in the paper boxes of neighborhoods in your area. I would target a neighborhood that you know has kids in the age range you are looking to tutor.

Also, I sent a few personal note cards and included my business cards to the department heads at schools in my area to let them know about my services and that helped me get referrals directly from teachers.

Q: Reading & math assessment?

*Posted by Rhonda on September 25 at 2:08 pm

I need some ideas for good reading and math assessments to give students anyone willing to share what you use

A: Reply by H. D. on September 25 at 10:41pm

I use Dr. Fry's reading assessments, although there are more thorough ones out there. These are quick and easy to give. I also use the Barton screener for students starting the Barton System, and the Math-U-See placement tests for math.

Reply by Tina on September 25 at 11:41pm

Generally I use the Fry assessments for reading, and if I think a more in-depth assessment is needed, I use DORA from Let's Go Learn (www.letsgolearn.com). DORA is a computer-based assessment that provides a parent and teacher report, as well as grade-level equivalents and strategies. The best math assessment I have found is the Excel Math placement tests (www.excelmath.com).

For older students who come in for pre-algebra and algebra, Let's Go Learn has excellent tests that split the skills into "strands" so that you know exactly what the student needs to work on. The Excel Math placement tests are free, and Let's Go Learn charges $20 per test, which I charge to the parent in addition to my regular fee. I know some tutors who like to give the Saxon math placement tests (free online), but I like the reasoning skills included in Excel. Hope this helps!

Reply by Lisa on September 26 at 9:24pm

Hi Rhonda,

I was introduced to DIBELS a few years ago. It is a reading assessment that is pretty quick to administer (although sometimes you have to take some time to go back to find the student's reading level). It goes up to grade 6. It targets fluency, comprehension, word attack, and phonemic awareness. I believe the materials are free on their website.

Q: Question about Tutoring Space

*Posted by Lisa on August 22 at 10:22pm

Hi all,

First, I want to say that this has been such a helpful forum, and I so much appreciate all the great insights and ideas I have gotten through it.

Next, I have a question about tutoring space... As it

turns out, my principal is going to allow me this coming year to work half days twice per week in order to have opportunity to grow my tutoring business. As it turns out, I feel like I'm starting to near capacity if I continue to drive to all my students' locations, and I realize I need to stick to one place to cut down on driving time. I am fortunate to have the opportunity of spare space my Dad has next to his office. It is small but will easily fit a 1:1 situation. However, it is on the second floor of an office building and there is no waiting area for parents. I am wondering if this may seem like an inconvenience to parents and be a deterrent for business, whether sticking to a library may be better. Still, it would be nice to have "my place"... you know? Any thoughts from those who may have experience with this? Thanks so much!

A: Reply by Lynda on September 1 at 10:39am

I think having a waiting area is an important aspect for your parents. Approximately 95% of the parents I work with wait while their child is being tutored. There are very few that drop off and pick up consistently for every session.

Reply by H. D. on September 4 at 4:36pm

I would agree a waiting area is essential, because you don't want parents just dropping off their kids. They may not come back on time, and then your whole schedule is messed up for the rest of that day, because you'll be stuck babysitting that kid until the parent shows up.

Q: Initial meeting with parents?

*Posted by Betty on September 9 at 4:21pm

A: Reply by Lynda on September 11 at 12:09am

I always start out by asking the parent what's going on with their child in terms of their learning concerns. Even if we discussed it over the phone, I make sure that I start out the conversation with the parent sharing about their child. I listen and take brief notes, asking questions when appropriate and needed. Then, I ask if they brought recent report cards, testing results, psychological tests, IEP, etc. then ask questions about those.

Then I give them my Parent Packet, (for more info visit www.tutoringprofits.com) which includes all the information they need to answer all the questions they may have. I walk them through the packet showing them the paperwork they need to complete. I answer any questions they have, then the parent(s) go fill out the paperwork in the waiting room while I begin the initial assessment with the student. (I only do about 30 minutes of the initial reading assessment. The tutor who I assign to the student completes the assessment during the first tutoring session. This gives the tutor time to get to know the student and experience their reading skills as well.) I start with the most basis reading assessment items such as letter/sound correspondences, then gradually move to harder assessment items such as phonemic awareness, and reading grade level passages.

After the assessment I bring the parent back in from the waiting room and review the results of the assessment with them. Next, I schedule the student for their tutoring sessions then collect the complete paperwork and the check.

The first meeting usually takes about 70-90 minutes:
1) 15-20 minutes for parent interview;
2) 30 minutes for beginning the student's reading assessment;
3) 15-20 minutes to present initial findings of the reading assessment to the parent.

Q: Reporting for Parents?
*Posted by H. D. on February 20 at 2:51pm

Hi all,
One thing I know I don't do enough as a tutor is give

meaningful, data-driven feedback to my parents. I do mostly Barton System Orton-Gillingham tutoring, but also some of my clients have been for writing skills, handwriting, and study skills. I was wondering if anyone has tips on some sort of assessment that can be quickly & easily given that I can use to show progress. Almost all of my clients have ADHD and do poorly on most standardized tests, and I don't want to add anything that creates unnecessary pressure for them.

Also, how often do you send emails reporting on student progress? I used to log what we did in every lesson and how the lesson went, and then send that as an excel file, but I don't think any of my parents actually read it- also it was time-consuming. I am thinking of just writing weekly or bi-weekly summaries & sending it as an email.

A: Reply by Dr. Alicia on February 21 at 4:36pm

I think parents want to know what is going on in

sessions and maybe you could provide notes to the parents after two sessions to let them know how they are progressing. When I started tutoring, it was very time consuming, but the notes really did help. Recently, I just found a new way to take notes-- using my SmartPen. Here's the URL: http://www.livescribe.com/en-us/

The information that is written in your own handwriting can be translated to the computer in whatever format that you desire and can easily send notes to the parents in no time. This has been a blessing to my tutoring business and do not leave home without it.

Reply by Kasey Hammond on February 21 at 5:40pm

I send a summary after each session and email it to parent(s). It is a little time consuming but I use my notes also for myself before meeting with the students the following week so it benefits me too. I normally schedule a few sessions at a time and don't always have time to chat with parents after meeting with their student for a long time so this helps chatting for a long time after a session too.

Reply by Latonya on February 23 at 8:58pm

I send monthly handwritten notes. I have carbon copy progess reports. I write out the goals for the particular month at the beginning of the month, and by the end of the month I document improvements, comments, etc. I do add to the reports before the end of the month arrives. My parents actually do not ask for notes, but I try to give them the reports each month. So far monthly reports have worked for me.

Closing thoughts...

Thank you again for purchasing my book. I have written this from my experience of being a tutor over the last 6 years. I hope this book will help you either begin your own tutoring business or, if you already have your own business provide you with more ideas, tools and suggestions to implement into your successful business!

Thank you!

GOOD LUCK & HAPPY TUTORING!

Kasey Hammond

www.YourTutoringBusiness.com

NOTES:

Made in the
USA
Middletown, DE